THE DAY GABBY DOUGLAS WON GOLD

by Ellen **Aim**

Creative Media, Inc.
PO Box 6270
Whittier, California 90609-6270
United States of America

If you purchased this book without a cover, you should be aware that this book is stolen property. It was reported as "unsold and destroyed" to the publisher, and neither the author nor the publisher has received any payment for this "stripped book."

The scanning, uploading, and distribution of this book via the Internet or via any other means without the permission of the publisher is illegal and punishable by law. Please purchase only authorized electronic editions and do not participate in or encourage electronic piracy of copyrighted materials. Your support of the authors' rights is appreciated.

The publisher does not have any control and does not assume any responsibility for author or third-party website or their content.

www.creativemedia.net

Book & cover design by Joseph Dzidrums

Copyright © 2016 by Creative Media, Inc. All rights reserved.
Printed in the United States of America.

First Edition: May 2016

LCCN: On File
ISBN: 978-1-938438-86-8
eISBN: 978-1-938438-87-5

In the all-around event, each gymnast competes on every apparatus: Vault, Uneven Bars, Balance Beam, and Floor Exercise. In the end, the athlete who posts the highest point total wins the gold medal.

It began as a dream...
July 31, 2012

In the summer of 2004, eight-year-old Gabby Douglas dreamed of winning gymnastics' Olympic all-around gold medal. As she watched Carly Patterson nab the title, she imagined herself winning it one day, too. After all, she was a gymnast just like Carly!

Eight years later, Gabby led the American girls' gymnastics squad to a team gold medal. As she celebrated the victory with her teammates, sports fans were already looking ahead to the next event.

In two days, Gabby would compete for the gold medal in the individual all-around competition. Could she make her childhood dream come true?

August 2, 2012
Two days later...

Wearing Team USA's standard uniform, Gabby Douglas waited by the sidelines for the all-around competition to begin. With Coach Liang Chow by her side, the sixteen-year-old felt confident and ready.

Gabby closed her eyes and pictured her dreams coming true. The determined gymnast imagined herself standing on the top step of the podium wearing the gold medal.

When Gabby opened her eyes, she felt ready to compete.

Gabby's shiny leotard lined with silver sequins sparkled under the bright lights. She looked like a superstar.

The gymnast eyed her first all-around event: the vault. She sprinted powerfully down the runway toward the apparatus. Seconds later, the confident gymnast soared through the air and landed with only a small hop. The crowd roared. She had just completed gymnastics' most difficult vault.

15.966

1st place with 3 rounds to go!

Hang time!

Gabby hurried to event two, the uneven bars. The apparatus once scared her, but it was now her favorite event. She flew so high in the air during her routines that people called her The Flying Squirrel.

Gabby applied chalk to her hands. She closed her eyes again and imagined herself performing a great routine.

That's exactly what happened!

Gabby soared through the air after hitting tricky release moves. She swung mightily from bar to bar while showing crisp, clean lines. When the teenager landed her difficult dismount, she beamed and ran to the sidelines to hug Coach Chow.

15.733

1st place with 2 rounds to go!

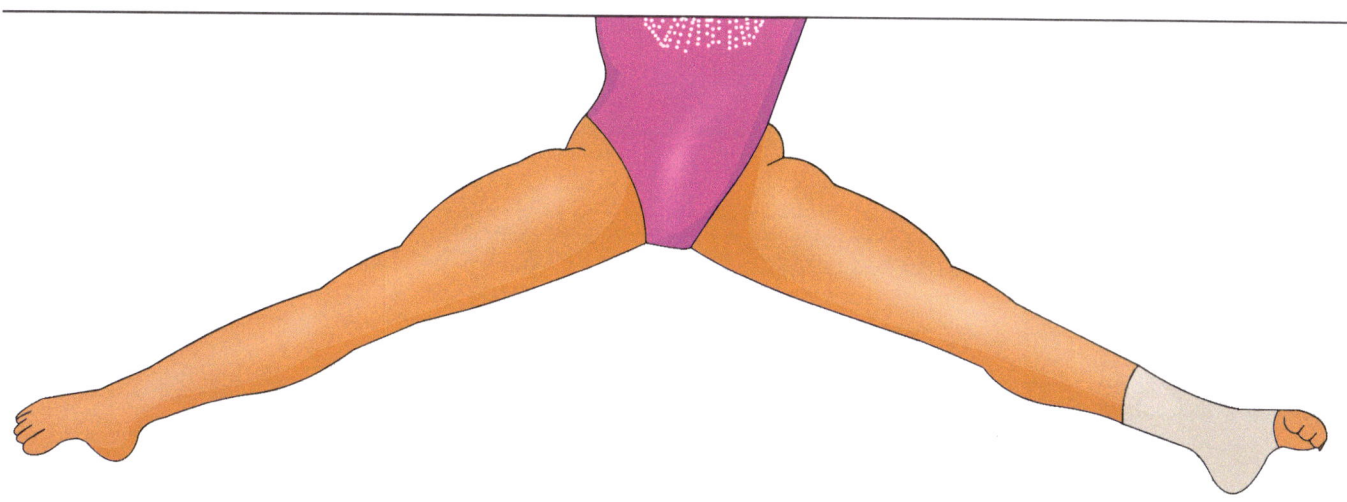

Gabby walked to the risky balance beam. She pictured herself performing a crowd-pleasing routine on the 3.9-inch wide apparatus. Tumbling on the tricky beam was always scary. Now, millions watched her every move.

Still, Gabby wanted that Olympic all-around medal. She would not lose sight of her dream.

In the end, she completed a graceful routine with solid tumbling! She grinned widely after the strong effort.

15.500

1st place with 1 round to go!

One final program stood between Gabby and gold. She took her starting position for her floor exercise routine. A good performance would keep her in first place.

When her music began, Gabby tumbled powerfully across the floor. She felt determined to make her dream come true.

Gabby loved her floor exercise program. The teenager had selected the catchy music believing the audience would adore it as much as she did. She was right. The crowd cheered wildly and clapped along with the upbeat tempo.

Gabby had loved performing in front of crowds since she was a little girl competing in small club events. Now she was having the time of her life at the Olympic Games while the world watched!

Gabby completed three successful tumbling runs in her program. If she landed the fourth one, she would probably win the all-around gold medal.

When it came time to complete the final tumbling pass, Gabby took a deep breath. Then, she unleashed a challenging acrobatic series.

When her music ended, Gabby smiled triumphantly. She had performed her best at the Olympics. It was a dream come true.

Gabby ran to Coach Chow and threw her arms around him in joy. Her hug thanked him for his never-ending encouragement and support over the years.

Coach Chow smiled proudly. The quiet man congratulated Gabby on four great performances. He felt so proud of his star student.

After the competition ended, Gabby held her breath while awaiting the final results. The American smiled nervously as cameras surrounded her. Finally, the scoreboard flashed the final standings.

1. Gabby Douglas United States
2. Viktoria Komova Russia
3. Aliya Mustafina Russia

Gabby was golden! The new Olympic champion cried joyful tears while waving to the crowd. The tiny powerhouse had won her second gold medal in two days.

Thanks to her Olympic success, Gabby Douglas became the first African American woman to win the all-around title. She was also the first female gymnast to capture gold in the team and individual events in the same Olympics.

After Gabby accepted her gold medal, she smiled broadly and waved to the adoring crowd. The pensive athlete thought of all the sacrifices she and her family had made over the years to reach her dream. Moments later, she sang softly as "The Star-Spangled Banner" played throughout the arena.

Gabby Douglas became an overnight celebrity after the Olympics. The popular athlete signed many commercial, television, and book deals. *Lifetime Television* even released a movie based on her life story!

Although Gabby Douglas owned two Olympic gold medals, she still had many dreams. The popular athlete dreamed of becoming an actress. She dreamed of going to college one day. She dreamed of competing at the 2016 Olympics. She dreamed of starting a foundation that would encourage young female athletes.

Why does Gabby still dream like the rest of us? Because dreams are never-ending.

Timmy
And the Baseball Birthday Party

Meet 4½ year old Timmy Martin! He's the biggest baseball fan in the world.

Imagine Timmy's excitement when he gets invited to his cousin's birthday party. Only it's not just any old birthday party... It's a baseball birthday party!

Timmy and the Baseball Birthday Party is the first book in a series of stories featuring the world's most curious little boy!

Quinn the Ballerina
The Sleeping Beauty!

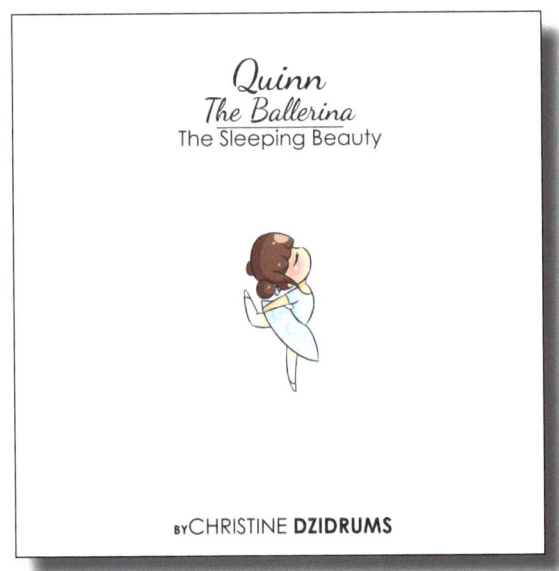

Quinn the Ballerina can hardly believe it's finally performance day. She's playing her first principal role in a production of *The Sleeping Beauty*.

Yet, Quinn is also nervous. Can she really dance the challenging steps? Will people believe her as a cursed princess caught in a 100-year spell?

Join Quinn as she transforms into Princess Aurora in an exciting retelling of Tchaikovsky's *The Sleeping Beauty*. Now you can relive, or experience for the first time, one of ballet's most acclaimed works as interpreted by a 9 year old.

Winning Silver

I'm Soooo Bored!
Minecraft Edition

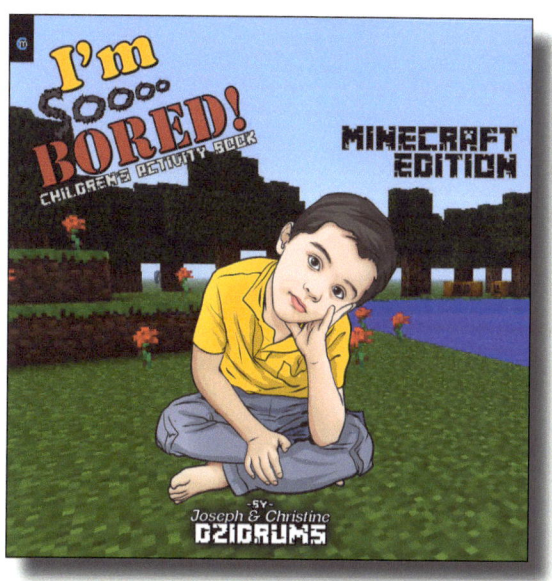

What happens when Elise delivers perfect routines but doesn't win? Can the disappointed gymnast accept the silver medal when she dreamed only of gold?

Filled with adorable illustrations and armed with straightforward storytelling, **Winning Silver** stresses the importance of good sportsmanship. Anyone who has ever felt gutted by a competitive result will relate to Elise's initial disappointment over not getting the result she expected.

Erase your child's boredom and stir their attention – away from the computer and television!

Packed with exiting, educational projects, *I'm Soooo Bored! Minecraft Edition* will entertain your child for hours without them ever needing a computer, tablet, or television. Imagine that!

Fair Youth
Emylee of Forest Springs

Twelve-year-old Emylee Markette has felt invisible her entire life. Then one fateful afternoon, three beautiful sisters arrive in her sleepy New England town and instantly become the most popular girls at Forest Springs Middle School. To everyone's surprise, the Fay sisters befriend Emylee and welcome her into their close-knit circle. Before long, the shy loner finds herself running with the cool crowd, joining the track team and even becoming friends with her lifelong crush.

Through it all, though, Emylee's weighed down by nagging suspicions. Why were the Fay sisters so anxious to befriend her? How do they know some of her inner thoughts? What do they truly want from her?

When Emylee eventually discovers that her new friends are secretly fairies, she finds her life turned upside down yet again and must make some life-changing decisions.

Fair Youth: Emylee of Forest Springs marks the first volume in an exciting new book series.

Future Presidents Club
Girls Rule!

Ashley Moore wants to know why there's never been a girl president. Before long the inspired six-year-old creates a special, girls-only club - the **Future Presidents Club**. Meet five enthusiastic young girls who are ready to change the world. ***Future Presidents Club: Girls Rule*** is the first book in a series about girls making a difference!

Princess Dessabelle Makes a Friend

Build Your GymnStars™ Collection Today!

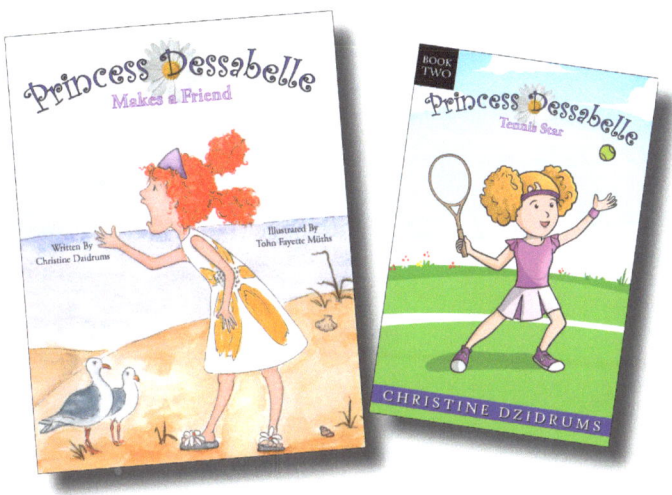

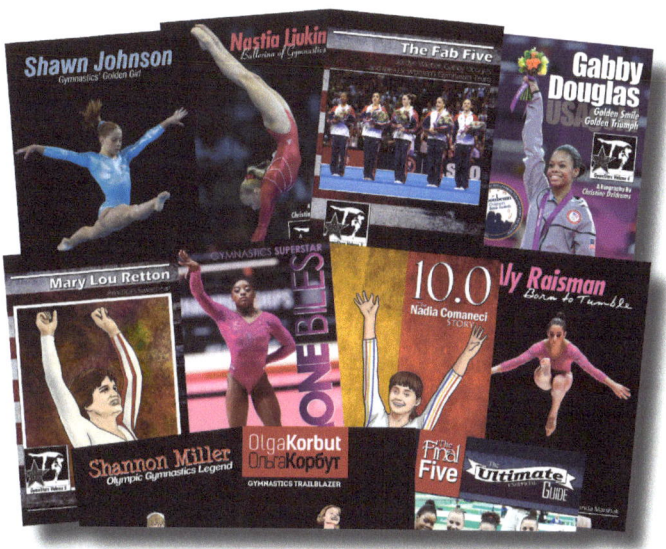

Meet **Princess Dessabelle**, a spoiled, lonely princess with a quick temper.

In *Princess Dessabelle Makes a Friend*, the lonely youngster discovers the meaning of true friendship. *Princess Dessabelle: Tennis Star* finds the pampered girl learning the importance of good sportsmanship.

Now sports fans can learn about gymnastics' greatest stars! Americans **Shawn Johnson** and **Nastia Liukin** became the darlings of the 2008 Beijing Olympics when the fearless gymnasts collected 9 medals between them. Four years later at the 2012 London Olympics, America's **Fab Five** claimed gold in the team competition. A few days later, **Gabby Douglas** added another gold medal to her collection when she became the fourth American woman in history to win the Olympic all-around title. The *GymnStars* series reveals these gymnasts' long, arduous path to Olympic glory. *Gabby Douglas: Golden Smile, Golden Triumph* received a **2012 Moonbeam Children's Book Award**.

Y Not Girl™
Women Who Inspire!

Our **YNot Girl** series chronicles the lives and careers of the world's most famous role models. **Jennie Finch: Softball Superstar** details the California native's journey from a shy youngster to softball's most famous face. In **Kelly Clarkson: Behind Her Hazel Eyes**, young readers will find inspiration reading about the superstar's rise from a broke waitress with big dreams to becoming one of the recording industry's top musical acts. **Missy Franklin: Swimming Sensation** narrates the Colorado native's transformation from a talented swimming toddler to queen of the pool.

StageStars™
Broadway's Best!

Theater fans first fell for **Sutton Foster** in her triumphant turn as *Thoroughly Modern Millie*. Since then the triple threat has charmed Broadway audiences by playing a writer, a princess, a movie star, a nightclub singer, and a Transylvania farm girl. Now the two-time Tony winner is conquering television in the acclaimed series *Bunheads*. A children's biography, **Sutton Foster: Broadway Sweetheart, TV Bunhead** details the role model's rise from a tiny ballerina to the toast of Broadway and Hollywood.

Idina Menzel's career has been "Defying Gravity" for years! With starring roles in *Wicked* and *Rent*, the Tony-winner is one of theater's most beloved performers. The powerful vocalist has also branched out in other mediums. She has filmed a recurring role on television's smash hit *Glee* and lent her talents to the Disney films, *Enchanted* and *Frozen*. A children's biography, **Idina Menzel: Broadway Superstar** narrates the actress' rise to fame from a Long Island wedding singer to overnight success!

www.ingramcontent.com/pod-product-compliance
Lightning Source LLC
Chambersburg PA
CBHW040021050426
42452CB00002B/83